*** Vietnam * The Habit of War ***

Robert Archer

Catholic Institute for International Relations, 22 Coleman Fields, London N1 7AF, UK.

Hanoi.

Acknowledgment
CIIR would like to thank Gil Loescher of the Department of Government, University of Notre Dame, Indiana, for his help in the writing of this booklet.

First published in October 1983 by
Catholic Institute for International Relations, 22 Coleman Fields, London N1 7AF, UK.
© CIIR 1983

Vietnam: The Habit of War
Archer, Robert
Vietnam
1. Vietnam — History — 20th century
I. Title
959.704   DS556.9

ISBN 0 904393 68 2

Copies available by post from CIIR. Trade distribution to bookshops and library supplies by Third World Publications, 151 Stratford Road, Birmingham B11 1RD, Tel. 021-773 6572

Printed by the Russell Press Ltd, Betrand Russell House, Nottingham (UK).
Design by Jan Brown Designs, London

Contents

Map of Vietnam

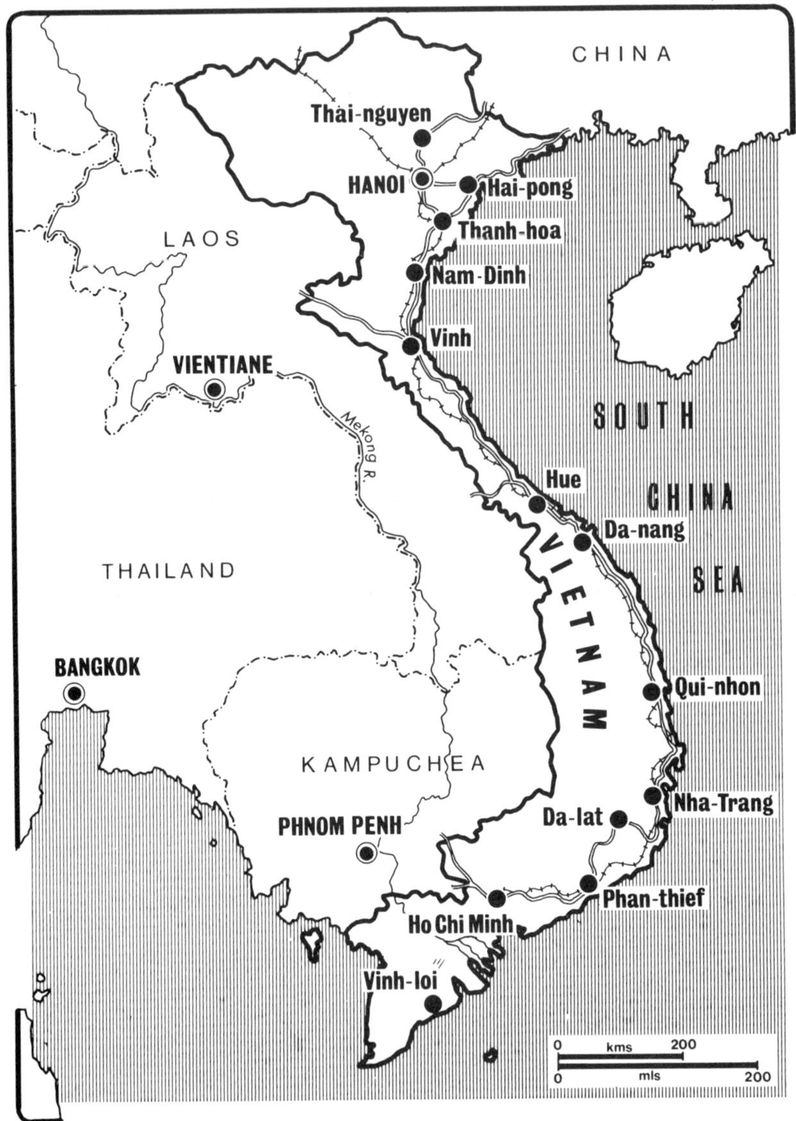

Introduction

Between 1945 and 1975, the Vietnam war—which engulfed Kampuchea (Cambodia) and Laos as well as Vietnam itself—dominated regional politics in South-East Asia. During three decades of hostilities, countless lives were lost in a struggle which symbolised the aspirations of Third World peoples for national independence and, at the same time, the global competition for influence waged by communist and non-communist powers in Asia.

Since 1979, regional politics have once more been dominated by Indo-China, this time by the tragedy of Kampuchea and the contested presence in that country of 150,000 Vietnamese troops. It is now recognised that while it governed Kampuchea between 1975 and 1978, the communist 'Khmer Rouge' regime of Pol Pot used extraordinary violence against its own population. Hundreds of thousands, some argue as many as two million, died. In early 1979, following serious border conflicts between the two countries, the regime was overturned by the Vietnamese army, which installed a government more favourable to it. This regime, led since 1981 by Heng Samrin, has not been recognised internationally. The countries of ASEAN (the Association of South East Asian Nations, composed of Thailand, Malaysia, Singapore, Indonesia and the Philippines), supported by the United States and by member governments of the EEC, have called upon Vietnam to withdraw its troops from Kampuchea, and permit the election of an independent and neutral government. The General Assembly of the United Nations has supported this demand.

In place of the Heng Samrin government, a coalition of three opposition movements—the Coalition Government of Kampuchea—is accredited at the United Nations. It is composed of the Khmer Rouge—by far the most powerful force, still in control of several thousand men under arms, The People's National Liberation Front, led by an ex-Prime Minister, Son Sann, and the Moulinaka faction of Norodom Sihanouk, who, as Prince Sihanouk, governed Cambodia as a neutral and independent state until 1970 when he was toppled by a coup d'état supported by the United States. The coalition is armed by the People's Republic of China, which has been the Khmer Rouge's principal ally since 1975, and to a lesser extent by the governments of ASEAN. In early 1979 China briefly invaded Vietnam's northern provinces in retaliation for its assault against the Khmer Rouge.

The Socialist Republic of Vietnam, meanwhile, remains on a war footing. With over one million men under arms, it now has the third largest army in the world, and stations some 150,000 to 180,000 soldiers in Kampuchea, with another 40,000 in Laos, which is today virtually a Vietnamese satellite. A further 20,000 troops, in addition to a larger number of militia, are based along Vietnam's northern border with China, which has remained tense since the Chinese incursion of 1979. In conflict with its erstwhile ally to the north, militarily engaged in both Kampuchea and Laos, politically at odds with the non-communist neighbouring states of ASEAN, Vietnam is internationally isolated; the Western world condemns its policies and, led by the United States, has imposed strict economic sanctions. As a result, it has come to rely increasingly upon close military and economic ties with the Soviet Union. For the same reason, the Vietnamese government has fostered and reinforced a tripartite alliance with Kampuchea and Laos in which Vietnam is clearly the dominant partner.

Vietnam refuses to withdraw from Kampuchea for

reasons of its own security. It claims that, if it did so, the Khmer Rouge would once again seize power, and would not only attack Vietnam as they did between 1975 and 1978, but would terrorise the Kampuchean people. The Vietnamese government's assessment of the Khmer Rouge as one of the most authoritarian and brutal regimes of modern history is widely shared. Most observers also agree that it is militarily the most effective of the three opposition movements within the Coalition Government of Kampuchea.

At the same time, observers have expressed mounting alarm at the evidence of stagnation, increased debt and real poverty within Vietnam itself. The Vietnamese economy was massively damaged during the war with America. Much of the damage was long term. Today Vietnam has one of the lowest standards of living in the world. The immense problems of reconstruction have been exacerbated by natural disasters, mistaken policies under the Second Five Year Plan (1976-1980) and general mismanagement and corruption. In addition, the government spends a high proportion of its budget on defence. Many believe that the economic prospects are little short of catastrophic and that the continuing exodus of refugees is a tragic and visible sign of this. Since 1979 the United States and its allies, including Britain and the EEC, have imposed an embargo on almost all development and humanitarian aid. This means, in practice, that the people of Vietnam continue to be deprived of essential resources, including basic medicines, educational materials and food, of which they are in acute need.

Map of the Region

1. History: The War 1945-75

It is difficult to over-estimate the influence of the war on political attitudes in Vietnam or on the country's economic prospects. Nor can current relations between Kampuchea and Vietnam be understood without reference to the region's long, troubled history.

Traditional relations between the two countries have been hostile, as have those between Vietnam and China, which has frequently invaded, and for long periods governed, it. Northern Vietnam formed part of the Chinese empire from the second century BC until 939 AD, when the Vietnamese successfully ended direct Chinese rule. Between 1406 and 1427 Ming dynasty troops invaded Vietnam again, and yet another Chinese expeditionary force, the last before imposition of French rule in the 19th century, was defeated in 1789. Over the same period Vietnamese people spread both westwards and southwards along the coast towards the Mekong delta, absorbing or expelling by war other peoples and kingdoms in their progress. Most of Champa, founded in 192 AD and centred in the lower Mekong valley, and much of the ancient Khmer kingdom were absorbed in this way, and Kampucheans are acutely aware of the long record of Vietnamese colonialism in their country.

Vietnamese expansion westwards was conditioned by

several factors, of which physically the most important was the Annamite chain of mountains running parallel to the coast, which defines the shape of modern Vietnam. Many of the hill peoples in the mountain areas (Hmong, Yao, Tia 'Pou Thai' and others) never accepted Vietnamese (or French) authority and created a line of buffer zones between the Vietnamese and other states in the region. Nevertheless, the Vietnamese did expand into this region and competed with the local peoples for sovereignty and living space in the area covered by modern Laos, Kampuchea and the Western provinces of Thailand, where various kingdoms were at different times under Khmer (Cambodian), Siamese (Thai) or Vietnamese suzerainty. European colonial rule imposed fixed borders in the 20th century.

Colonialism and Resistance

French colonisation of Indo-China in the 19th century temporarily re-ordered historic patterns of regional conflict. France seized Saigon in 1858-59, officially to protect Catholic missions in the area, but chiefly to establish a naval base. After several attempts between 1873 and 1883, France took Hanoi and in 1885 established control over all of modern Vietnam, which the French divided into three areas: Tonkin, (North), Annam (Centre) and Cochin-China (South). By 1895, France had obtained possession of modern Laos (whose rulers had traditionally acknowledged both Vietnamese and Thai suzerainty), and modern Kampuchea.

Colonisation both arrested direct Vietnamese and Thai expansion into Kampuchea and at the same time accelerated the process by which Vietnamese acquired influence west of the Annamite chain and in the lower Mekong valley. With French encouragement, large numbers migrated into Kampuchea to work on plantations, and France employed many Vietnamese as civil servants in its administration of Kampuchea.

France and Britain were swept out of Asia by Japan in the second world war, and this, along with the rise of

Vietnamese nationalism, recreated throughout Indo-China a situation of tension which the colonial period had concealed but left unchanged. During most of the war Admiral Decoux was allowed by Japan to govern French Indo-China, on condition that he did not act contrary to Japanese interests; Japan exercised direct rule in Vietnam only for a very short period in 1945.

The Indo-China Communist Party was formed in 1930 by Ho Chi Minh, and took responsibility for the whole of Indo-China; separate sister parties in Laos and Cambodia were not created until 1951. In 1941 Ho Chi Minh led the party into an alliance, in which it was the major partner, within the Vietnam Independence League (or Vietminh), an anti-colonial nationalist movement. With American logistical support, the Vietminh fought against the Japanese until their surrender in 1945. In an attempt to repossess Indo-China, the French opened hostilities against the Vietminh in the same year, although American policy at this time was in favour of making some concessions to Vietnamese nationalism.

The Anti-Communist War

For the American government, however, the 'loss' of China to the communists in 1949 transformed the French Indo-China war from a colonial into an anti-communist struggle. Over the next quarter of a century, the United States committed itself militarily and politically to maintaining non-communist regimes in Indo-China, even though these were neither representative nor elected, and generally corrupt and ineffectual.

The first Indo-China war proved traumatic for French colonial policy. Between 1946 and 1954 172,000 French soldiers were killed. Talks were not convened in Geneva until 1954, when they coincided with the massive defeat of French troops at Dien Bien Phu near the Laos border. By this time the United States, already deeply involved in Korea, was bearing 70% of France's military costs.

At the Geneva talks, over which Britain and the USSR

14

jointly presided, the Vietminh agreed to the temporary partition of Vietnam at the 17th parallel. They did so under pressure from both Peking and Moscow, on the understanding that supervised elections would be held in 1956 to elect a national representative government.

In South Vietnam the Americans gave their support to Ngo Dinh Diem, and subsequently, after his assassination in a military coup in 1963, to a series of military governments with no popular political base, but a commitment to anti-communism. Diem and the Americans resisted implementation of the accords, particularly the election provisions. The Diem government's abuses, and the repression of communist cadres in the South, persuaded Hanoi to resume the war in 1959. Over the next decade and a half, as the war escalated, Laos and Cambodia as well as Vietnam were engulfed in the conflict.

The End of the War

By the late 1960s it had become clear that American attempts to impose a military solution in Vietnam were no more successful than those of France, and from 1968 new negotiations were opened in Paris between the United States, the Republic of [South] Vietnam (RVN), the Democratic Republic of [North] Vietnam (DRV) and the Provisional Revolutionary Government [of South Vietnam] (PRG). The United States imposed a policy of 'Vietnamisation' in the South, by which American troops were gradually replaced by South Vietnamese conscripts; in return, the United States greatly increased its military and economic aid to the Republic of Vietnam, by then led by General Nguyen Van Thieu.

By this period, after the Soviet invasion of Czechoslovakia in 1968 and the escalation of Sino-Soviet tension during the summer of 1969, Peking had come to believe that the Soviet Union rather than the United States was China's principal external threat, and Chinese leaders began working to secure a tactical accommodation with the

United States. China dropped its opposition to a negotiated settlement in Vietnam. In fact, both Moscow and Peking saw advantages in ending the war, and Hanoi came under considerable pressure from its allies to reach a settlement. It was during this period that the Nixon administration began to bomb Hanoi and Haiphong intensively, extending the war into Cambodia and Laos. Border regions were massively bombed. In Cambodia the neutral government of Prince Norodom Sihanouk was overturned in 1970 by a military coup and the regime of Lon Nol, supported and armed by the United States, intensified its war against the guerrillas of the Khmer Rouge, themselves supplied and supported by the government of North Vietnam. A similar if less dramatic escalation occurred in Laos, which was bombed by the United States even more intensively than Vietnam and Cambodia.

The Paris accords, signed in 1973, provided for the withdrawal of American military support for the South Vietnamese government, but did not end military hostilities. The war continued, at a terrible cost to the peoples of Vietnam, Laos and Cambodia, until April 1975, when the Thieu regime suddenly collapsed. Thirteen days earlier, Phnom Penh, the capital of Cambodia, had fallen to the Khmer Rouge. After almost thirty years of continuous, intense war, South and North Vietnam were united in a single Socialist Republic of Vietnam.

2. Government: The Socialist Republic of Vietnam

The Vietnamese Communist Party

The Vietnamese Communist Party is unique among communist governments in several respects. Its leadership's record of continuity is unrivalled; many leaders became prominent during the 1930s, and have only begun recently to make way for younger men since the 1979 Plenum and the Fifth Party Congress in February 1982. At Central Committee level, the party has always governed by consensus: this has permitted the leadership to remain united through major policy changes, for example, after the failure of the agricultural reform policy of the 1950s, and also at the present time. Neither during the war nor since has the Vietnamese Communist Party resorted to physical purges of the leadership to settle internal political disputes. On the other hand, opposition groups have been liquidated on occasion; several thousand landowners were killed during the land reform programme mentioned above. Nevertheless, no revenge killing took place after the victory of 1975, and the absence of violence after such a war stands as one of the outstanding achievements of the present government.

In foreign policy, while steadily loyal to its communist

allies, notably the Soviet Union, the Vietnamese Communist Party has also preferred to maintain friendly relations with as wide a range of countries as possible, including capitalist countries. It is the only country in the Council for Mutual Economic Assistance (CMEA, also known as COMECON) which is also a member of the IMF and the World Bank.

The Political System

Constitutionally, the highest authority in Vietnam is the State Council, a collective presidency which is answerable to a National Assembly elected by universal adult suffrage every five years. The National Assembly is the legislative authority and elects members to the State Council and the Council of Ministers, in whom executive power is vested. Government authority at district, ward and village level lies with People's Committees, answerable to People's Councils which are themselves elected with four-year mandates.

Judicial power is vested in a Supreme People's Court and in local People's Tribunals and Military Tribunals. These organisations have power of arrest, along with the security service and the People's Procuratorate, which also has a duty to monitor the judicial system.

Nevertheless Vietnam is governed officially according to Marxist-Leninist principles, and the Vietnamese Communist Party is the central and dominant political institution in the country. Article 2 of the Vietnamese constitution of 1981 states that 'The Socialist Republic of Vietnam is a State of proletarian dictatorship,' while Article 4 states that 'The Communist Party of Vietnam, the vanguard and general staff of the Vietnamese working class, armed with Marxism-Leninism, is the only force leading the State and society, and the main factor determining all successes of the Vietnamese revolution.'

Political Control

The party has wide powers of control in all areas of social and economic life. The circulation of books is carefully controlled;

18

the movement of individuals is restricted and travel passes are required even for short journeys. Non-communist organisations, such as churches, have the right to exist, but may not engage in political activity (Article 68), as defined by the government; independent political activity is not permitted. Political surveillance is explicit and widespread. The security apparatus has grown increasingly powerful within the state, although there is little evidence of physical repression, or torture. Those considered to be politically unreliable are monitored by local party organisations as well as by the police; they are often harassed. In general, the government and the party evaluate political reliability in the narrowest of terms and consider all except those who have embraced the language and style of the new regime as potential dissidents. According to the constitution (Article 4), the party 'exists and struggles for the interests of the working class and the people of Vietnam as a whole', but critics of the regime deny that the Party today represents, or is accountable to, the people. Ideological preconceptions deeply colour political debate about the government's record.

This is acutely true within Vietnam itself. Half the population has been familiar with the present government since 1954. However, those in the South have a completely different, capitalist experience and a higher standard of living. There is also a relatively large, literate middle class which greatly resents the extremely strict censorship which is currently imposed. Reconciliation was always a crucial challenge for the national government after 1975. It has not been met. Many Southerners disliked the Hanoi government on political grounds, but many who were uncommitted or sympathetic have since been disappointed by their lack of participation in the new system and angered by Hanoi's heavy-handed security controls. They claim that South Vietnam was not liberated in 1975, as promised, but conquered, and reject the doctrinaire policies which they feel have been imposed upon them. This has tended to create a vicious circle of mistrust. Increasing numbers of Vietnamese, particularly in the South, dare not voice their grievances for fear of arrest or political victimisation, while Hanoi, conscious of the degree of passive resistance to its rule, has

Repair of cyclone damage at the coast.

CIDSE — *Mayans*

tended to tighten its surveillance and impose ever more extensive security controls.

Many thousands of officials of the former South Vietnamese government and army, and former members of political parties and organisations that were classified as reactionary after 1975, have been imprisoned without trial in 're-education camps', and forced to learn new political attitudes. Among the detainees were active opponents of the Thieu regime. At least 16,000 are still held, some for seven years; often they have not been informed of the motive for their detention and sometimes their families do not know where they are. The camps are generally located in remote areas, are often unhealthy and lack electricity and running water. There is little evidence that detainees are physically maltreated. When freed, however, they have been denied civil rights, must provide the authorities with regular reports of their activities, cannot work without permission and have little freedom of movement.

Originally, the Vietnamese government promised that those held for 're-education' would be released within three years of the end of the war. The official reasons given for extending their detention have since shifted. The government now argues that Vietnam's national security would be threatened by the release of so many politically unreliable citizens. Amnesty International has condemned the 're-education' system as a fundamental violation of basic human rights.

The Government's New Economic Zone policy has also been criticised as repressive. It began as an attempt to meet the massive problems of overcrowding and unemployment at the end of the war. In the first year, 1976, 1.4 million people, mainly landless peasants and urban unemployed, were relocated in the South. One million returned to their villages, and 400,000 were settled on areas of previously uncultivated land called New Economic Zones. For both political and economic reasons, these ran into difficulty almost at once. Settlers faced severe hardship, owing to their own lack of agricultural experience and to the government's failure to supply water, tools, food and building materials as had been promised. Some NEZs lay in jungle, in marshland or on land too poor to yield crops. Thousands of Southerners deserted and slipped back into the urban areas.

When they did so, they discovered they were ineligible for work or rations; when found, they were threatened with arrest or return to the zones. It has become clear that the policy has not been used simply to cut urban unemployment. In recent years, those sent to NEZs have not only been the unemployed, but also former businessmen, civil servants or soldiers who had managed to remain in the cities.

Treatment of Dissidents

The Communist Party has moved to neutralise, or crush, other possible centres of dissidence. Prominent among those affected are religious groups. The leaders of the anti-communist Hoa Hao Buddhist sect in the Mekong Delta have been gaoled. The An Quang buddhist pagoda, a centre of militant opposition to the Thieu regime before 1975, has been shut and some of its members detained. Most religious publications have been obliged to close, including *Tin Sang*, Vietnam's last independent newspaper, which was launched by radical Catholics in 1975. According to Amnesty, in August 1983 at least 150 Catholic priests were believed to be detained or placed under house arrest. In the most recent trial, in June 1983, several Jesuits, including the regional Superior, Father Joseph Nguyên Công Doan, were sentenced to long periods of imprisonment. The evidence against them was insubstantial. The Jesuits in Vietnam have actively sought to accommodate government demands.

The Roman Catholic Church in Vietnam has recently been subjected to particularly close scrutiny. During the war period communication between Catholics in the North and South broke down. Those in the North, apart from being a minority, were also isolated from the changed Catholic approach to the modern world and secular state that grew out of the Second Vatican Council. They were entitled to practise their faith, on condition that they did not engage in politics, a position which on the whole they accepted.

In the South the church's experience was rather different. At partition in 1954 tens of thousands of Catholics left North Vietnam for the South to avoid falling under the control of the communist government and the Church became associated with support for the South Vietnamese government. At the same time, a minority of clergy and lay Catholics became increasingly critical of the corruption, violence and misgovernment of successive regimes in the South and, influenced by the new social awareness in the church, began working for greater social justice and respect for human rights. Some worked or sympathised with the National Liberation Front.

When Saigon fell in 1975, the Archbishop of Saigon opened the city's churches, hospitals and schools to the new government. The Catholic hierarchy's attitude at this time was described as one of the few pleasant surprises experienced by Hanoi. Relations were re-established between the bishops of North and South, who met for the first time in united council in 1981.

Relations between the Catholic Church and the government nevertheless remain sensitive. In general, the separate identity of religious groups — whether Christian or Buddhist — is seen by state and party institutions to be threatening and unacceptable. In addition, the emphasis placed on the social implications of faith have also made it more, rather than less, difficult for Catholics to withdraw from active involvement in the country's social and economic affairs. Finally, many Catholics, including some priests, undoubtedly sympathised with the old regime, while the Communist leadership appears to have conceived an exaggerated fear of a Catholic backlash after the rise of the dissident movement in Poland—even though the two million Catholics in Vietnam are only a small proportion of the population.

The Refugees

The refugee crisis which caught the world's attention after 1978 was caused partly by the oppressive climate created by government surveillance; but it was due as much to Vietnam's very severe economic difficulties and the political tension between China and Vietnam. The first waves of emigrants were composed of officials or officers of the South Vietnamese govenment; many of these people have continued to leave, often after release from detention camps. A second exodus, the most visible, was triggered by the hostility between China and Vietnam over Kampuchea. Between the spring of 1978 and July 1978, when China closed its border with Vietnam, more than 160,000 Vietnamese of Chinese ancestry travelled overland into China; another 70,000 left by ship. Over the following year, between mid-1978 and mid-1979, more than 500,000 fled—most, the so-called 'boat people', in small unseaworthy boats or overcrowded freighters. A small but rising proportion of the refugees have belonged to a third group, neither ex-officials nor Vietnamese of Chinese ancestry, but rural or urban working class Vietnamese, some of whom are escaping military service in Kampuchea.

It should be said that the great majority of the families of so-called Chinese Vietnamese have lived in Vietnam for one or several generations and are not recent immigrants from China.

Tens of thousands of the refugees have died en route or been murdered by pirates, and some vessels have been refused permission to land by the authorities in Malaysia, Singapore and Indonesia, where the scale of the exodus has caused serious reception difficulties. The number of refugees awaiting resettlement continues to pose a problem: there are now over 200,000 in the ASEAN countries and Hong Kong, many of whom have now been in camps for several years. Since host countries are increasingly reluctant to accept more refugees, their chances of resettlement are diminishing. Australia is virtually the only Western nation which has not yet cut its quota.

Corruption

Most of the refugees paid bribes of some US$2,000 to leave. There is evidence that the Vietnamese government tolerated or encouraged a harassment campaign against Vietnamese of Chinese descent, and that Vietnamese officials, some at high level, were directly involved in arranging illegal departures by boat. The trade probably earned a high proportion of Vietnam's foreign exchange during the period 1978-1980, when the country's economy was in ruins and the foreign currency reserves exhausted.

In fact, corruption is widespread, both in the North and in the South. Southern consumer goods, which are absent in the North, have proved irresistible to some Northern officials; but the crucial factors has been wide gap between the official and market values of the currency and the very low wages of public sector officials with fixed salaries. The one has created a parallel economy which is strongly entrenched, the other has forced officials to supplement their salaries either by bribes or outside entrepreneurial activity. Officials have so direct an interest in the black market that the resistance of middle cadres in the party to economic reforms is probably the principal obstacle to their effective introduction. In 1981 it was estimated that the average official wage of 80 dong a month was sufficient to buy on the open market one chicken and three kilos of rice (at 10 dong per kilo), in addition to the 13 kilos of rice officials were permitted to buy at the subsidised price of 0.40 dong per kilo. Since then, fixed wages have been doubled. Nevertheless there is widespread corruption, particularly among minor officials. The confusion between state and private interest is indicated by one report which suggested that only one-third of state-produced consumer goods were being distributed by the government; the rest were being siphoned off by officials for sale on the open market.

3. The Economy

The Effects of the War

The scale of Vietnam's economic problems in 1975 was described by the opening sentences of a World Bank report circulated during 1980:

> In the three decades following the end of the Second World War, almost every country has enjoyed substantial economic growth and an improvement in the welfare of its people . . . (But) when the war in Vietnam finally came to an end in 1975, per capita production of major commodities had changed little, or fallen, since the 1940s. Except in some parts of the South, the economic infrastructure is less well developed than in most developing countries and the country's standard of living is one of the lowest.

In addition to the basic problems of poverty or resource scarcity, the war had caused social dislocation on a staggering scale. At least 250,000 troops in the Southern army (as well as over 50,000 American soldiers) had lost their lives, while the number of communist military and civilian victims will never be known. It was possibly two million. The saturation bombing ordered by the American strategists ruined the North's infrastructure: American and South Vietnamese aircraft dropped on North Vietnam alone several times the tonnage of bombs used during the second world war. Roads, port facilities and industry were crippled, transport networks, fields and waterways heavily mined, the country' soil and forests extensively poisoned by defoliants. The intense use of high-technology warfare by the American military in Vietnam will have profoundly destructive effects upon Vietnam's agriculture and economic development for decades to come.

In addition to the estimated 1.5 million civilian casualties of the war, hundreds of thousands were crippled. By 1975, almost every family in the North and South had suffered the loss of relatives or their livelihood. The population of North Vietnam had to face the physical and psychological stress of saturation bombing over long periods, while American military occupation and insurgency profoundly disrupted social and economic structures in the South. About 16% of the population of South Vietnam were killed or wounded during the war, and between 1965 and 1976 57% were made homeless. Two entire generations of children were brought

up in these conditions. By 1975 there were between 800,000 and one million orphans—about 11% of the total number of South Vietnamese children under 15 years of age. Some had been fathered by American soldiers. Vast numbers of peasants abandoned their lands, either driven into the cities by the bombing and hostilities or attracted there by the hope of better living conditions, and also by the South Vietnamese government's own policies. The proportion of rural dwellers in the South dropped from 85% in 1966 to 35% of the population in 1975, while between 1972 and 1975 alone the population of Saigon swelled from 1.8 to 3.8 million. These massive transfers of refugees and migrants devastated the rural economy and generated an artificial urban lifestyle which had no autonomous economic base.

In fact the economies of both North and South were critically dependent upon foreign economic aid. The economy of the South was propped up by about US$2,000m. per year during the 1970s. This was used to support the budget and for military and project aid. The millions of refugees who swelled the cities and towns gained employment primarily through the American or South Vietnamese military

Construction of serum factory, Hanoi.

machines and their service industries, or lived unproductively from American economic assistance. Crime, drug trading and prostitution became endemic, administrative and financial corruption rampant. Although it had developed in a very different way and living standards remained very much lower, the Northern economy was arguably almost as dependent upon external assistance for the supply of food, transport, medicines—and of course arms. Perhaps half of North Vietnam's gross domestic product during the war was supplied by its allies. With these resources, central government planning had been able to provide almost all its citizens with basic social services in health and education, and in this area the government won international respect. Agriculture has been partially collectivised, but with much less success. No judgement is possible on North Vietnam's industrial achievement, because the country's plant was destroyed several times over.

The extreme economic contrast between the two societies compounded problems of adjustment that would have been severe under any circumstances. It added to other long-standing divisions in Vietnamese society, many of which stemmed from events of the past hundred years or more: divisions between Catholics and Buddhists, rich and poor, urban and rural dwellers, Westernised and non-Westernised Vietnamese, highland minorities and lowland villagers, government bureaucrats and those they governed.

Post-War Economic Policy

At the Fourth Party Congress in December 1976, the government emphasised the importance of restoring production, solving unemployment and preparing for the gradual imposition of state control over economic activity. Vietnam's Second Five Year Plan (1976-1980) gave priority to agriculture, first of all to meet the population's basic food requirements and then to provide raw materials for industrial development and export.

The plan failed disastrously either to restore production

Street market, Ho Chi Minh Ville.

and stimulate agriculture, or to reconcile North and South. Although in March 1978 over 30,000 businesses in South Vietnam were abruptly closed and private businessmen trading in goods under state control were asked to return to their villages or transfer to New Economic Zones, the authorities failed to check the resilient private sector in Ho Chi Minh City (Saigon). Efforts to collectivise landholding in the South ran into similar problems. By July 1979 some 13,000 production collectives had reportedly been formed in Ho Chi Minh City and twelve Southern provinces; but because of inadequate political groundwork, inadequate funds and incompetent cadres, many simply did not function. Peasant farmers were demoralised by poor farm prices, constantly rising agricultural taxes and the scarcity of consumer goods to buy with the earnings they did receive. The collectivisation programme was opposed so effectively by peasants in the South that rice production in the fertile Mekong valley, and sales of rice to the government, fell. Cereal production (including rice) rose by only 3% instead of the 54% planned for the first five year period, and official rations in the North were cut in 1980 to 13 kilos a month (2 fewer than the minimum recommended by the World Health Organisation). In addition, Vietnam had to contend with natural disasters which played havoc with the agricultural sector. Cold weather, drought and several typhoons caused crop failures in 1976 and 1977, and in 1978 Vietnam suffered the most severe flooding in its recent history. It became necessary to import large quantities of grain, mostly from the USSR. Soviet food aid reportedly reached a peak of 1.8 million tonnes in 1980, before the introduction of an incentive system caused cereal production to increase again.

Partly owing to pollution of the water systems during the war, fish catches also fell, from about 600 000 tons in 1976 to about 350 000 in 1980. Each Vietnamese consumed on average only 9.5 kilos of fish in 1980, compared with 16 kilos in 1976. Hardship was greatest among officials and other urban dwellers with fixed incomes, but farmers and agricultural producers also suffered. Until they were increased after the Sixth Plenum in 1979, state prices for food often bore no relation to production costs. Sugar cane,

CIDSE — Mayans

for example, was priced at 68 dong per tonne, although it cost farmers 220-250 dong to produce; shrimps — a valuable export commodity and an important element of diet — were purchased by the government at below fishermen's costs. As a result, many sugar mills were forced to close and exports of shrimp declined.

Transport problems have paralysed economic recovery. The facilities of Haiphong harbour, which carries 60% of Vietnam's external trade, have not been properly repaired since they were mined and bombed during the American war. Roads are in a similar or worse state, the railways need to be reconstructed and modernised and many navigable rivers and waterways have silted up. Industries are dependent upon imported raw materials which may be delayed in Haiphong for months or until they are unuseable. Vietnam's sugar mills have been working at 30% of capacity. In 1981 livestock food production stood at 18% of full output and tinned milk factories were down to 10% of possible turnover. Coal production also fell, a serious problem for the country's economy because 60% of Vietnam's electricity is produced by coal-fired power stations. Most of the country's petrol —

33

about 1.5 m. tonnes in 1979 — has been supplied by the USSR at subsidised prices. Finally, many factories, power stations and mines were destroyed by the Chinese army in 1979, which further aggravated shortages in some essential sectors.

Exports have fallen sharply in relation to imports. As a result, Vietnam's debt to the socialist bloc has soared, and its international trade outside CMEA has collapsed. Between 1978 and 1981, Vietnam earned less currency from trade outside CMEA than it needed simply to pay the interest charges on its foreign debt to Western countries. The interest charge rose from US$4m. a year in 1976 to US$24m. in 1977, US$204m. in 1980 and US$236m. in 1982 — a figure which represented some 56% of Vietnam's total export earnings and no less than 240% of its earnings outside CMEA in 1982.

By early 1981 the IMF estimated that Vietnam's total foreign debt amounted to some US$3bn. In that year, while goods worth US$369m. were exported, imports were valued at US$1.08bn; the figure improved relatively in 1982 — exports rising to US$430m. and imports falling to US$838m. — but these figures nevertheless mark the scale of Vietnam's current crisis and dependence upon aid. Reserves of hard currency were estimated in 1982 to be only US$10-16m. Except for one repayment of US$25m, the government has also defaulted on all repayments of its debt to the IMF, and has been obliged to seek agreement with its international creditors to reschedule interest payments on its loans.

The Reform Programme

The failure of the Second Five Year Plan gave rise to serious concern inside and outside the government and, beginning with the Sixth Plenum in late 1979, the party initiated a programme of economic, social and political reforms. Leadership changes were subsequently announced in the ministries handling various aspects of the country's economy, and important changes have taken place in the Central

Committee and the government. Older, sometimes less effective party and government officials were replaced by younger, more qualified, technocrats—although the great mass of middle-rank cadres who are responsible for executing policy at local level, and for much of Vietnam's bureaucratic inefficiency, remain at their posts. The economic reforms play down collectivisation and central planning and encourage more private initiative. The government has permitted farmers to sell their produce at free market prices, once they have provided the state with a fixed quota, which will not be raised until 1985, and traders have been encouraged to operate privately in sectors in which the state marketing system has proved incapable of assuring essential supplies at prices which reflect producers' costs. Family industry has also been given incentives, in an attempt to stimulate flagging production and maximise the use of resources. Furthermore, the South as a whole has been granted greater autonomy in its implementation of economic policy. Officials have admitted that this will lead to greater disparities between rich and poor, and between fixed income urban dwellers and rural farmers (who stand to benefit most from higher agricultural prices); also between the poorer North and the South.

The policy is provisional and has been introduced after considerable debate within the party; it is quite likely to be restricted or withdrawn. Nevertheless the first signs are that it has succeeded in raising production in many sectors. Exports in 1982 increased by 27% over the 1980 figure, coal extraction by 60%, and grain production rose 13% in 1981, and by another 8% in 1982 to 16.3 million tonnes. The government has announced that it hopes to achieve self-sufficiency in food by 1985—which would mean only that import imbalance will cease, not that individual consumption will necessarily increase. Indeed, the government expects a further decline in living standards as price controls are lifted and imports of food and other consumer commodities are reduced. There are severe problems of production, distribution and pricing to overcome, and although the slide into economic collapse appears to have been arrested, ordinary Vietnamese must still look forward to continued poverty. Development of the country's resources, and also provision for some of the people's basic needs — medicines, educational resources and food—will continue to depend upon aid or investment from abroad.

4. The Kampuchean War and the International Aid Embargo

The triumph of the Vietnamese, Kampuchean and Laotian communist parties in Indochina in 1975 did not lead to any unity in policy; indeed hostility between the government of Vietnam and the new government of Kampuchea increased. Their experience during both Indo-China wars led the Vietnamese leadership to believe that their security interests required the close alignment of Laos and Kampuchea. The 25-year treaty of friendship and cooperation signed with Vientiane in 1977 established Vietnamese influence in Laos, but the Khmer Rouge government resisted any such relationship for Kampuchea.

After 1975 in fact, one faction of the Khmer Rouge led by Pol Pot, suspicious of Vietnam's long-term intentions, murdered most of the Vietnamese or Vietnamese-trained members of the pro-Vietnamese faction within the Kampuchean Communist Party and initiated extremely savage cross-border raids into Vietnam. At the same time, there was a major re-alignment of policy among the powers directly interested in Indo-China. The end of the war in 1975 removed any remaining restraints imposed by the need for solidarity on Vietnam's allies, and rivalry between the communist powers became pronounced. While the Soviet Union increased its influence in Vietnam and promoted a security pact against China, Peking encouraged the nations of ASEAN to collaborate with each other and with the United States to oppose what it viewed as Soviet and Vietnamese expansion. The Soviet Union and China became respectively the external patrons of Vietnam and Kampuchea.

By 1978, the Vietnamese government had concluded that the Khmer Rouge regime was intolerable and endangered Vietnam's own security. In December the Vietnamese army invaded, overturned the Pol Pot regime—in so doing revealing to the world the extremity of suffering endured after 1975 by the Kampuchean people—and installed the present govenment, led since 1981 by Heng Samrin. Since then, Vietnam has strengthened the Indo-Chinese Federation of Laos, Kampuchea and Vietnam, which Vietnam dominates, and has resisted all claims to greater political autonomy for Kampuchea. For the Kampuchean people, at least in terms of personal survival and repression, Vietnamese occupation is a lesser evil than the Khmer Rouge. But it is not a solution. The presence in Kampuchea of Vietnamese advisers and the Vietnamese army prevents the people of Kampuchea from exercising their right to self-determination. Also, because it is regarded as unacceptable by China and by Vietnam's ASEAN neighbours, military occupation is unlikely to satisfy Vietnam's desire for long-term security along its extended Western frontier.

These political developments led directly to Vietnam's international isolation: they also harmed the country's economic prospects. Firstly, China retaliated by invading Vietnam's northern provinces, causing considerable damage. The New People's Army systematically destroyed mines, roads, factories, hospitals and other economic assets in the border area. The destruction of the phosphate mine at Lao Cai had especially harmful effects upon agriculture.

Secondly, Vietnam's hostile relations with its neighbours caused the Vietnamese government to reinforce its defence commitments. The size of the Vietnamese army, and the country's defence budget, increased after the American war ended in 1975. 150-180,000 troops — about 15% of the army—have been stationed in Kampuchea since 1979, while a much larger proportion is ranged permanently in combat readiness along the frontier with China. Military expenditure consumes a high proportion of the national budget. Defence costs increased so sharply in 1978, that the government chose to cut capital expenditure on development projects by some 30%. Vietnam's defence expenditure has also increased military dependence upon the Soviet Union, which supplies most of the arms the government acquires. Thus, the growing size of Vietnam's military establishment and its presence in Laos and Kampuchea, have helped create a regional arms spiral, expensive to all the nations concerned.

Thirdly, Vietnam's military occupation of Kampuchea, and the failure to resolve the international controversy over that country's status, caused the ASEAN states, Japan, Australia, the United States, most countries in Europe including the EEC, and China, to end bilateral aid programmes to Vietnam. The United States has also lobbied with some success to cut the international agencies' aid allocations for Vietnam.

The Aid Embargo

It is estimated that non-communist aid to Vietnam between 1975 and 1978 amounted to more than US$2bn, of which some US$740m. was in the form of grants; over the same period international agencies also provided some US$625m. in assistance. Of this amount, developing countries provided a sizeable proportion, about US$1bn, of which India alone contributed US$77m; the Middle East oil-producing countries (Iraq, Libya and Kuwait in particular) loaned about US$700m. at low interest rates for oil purchases. Chinese aid was also considerable until 1978. During the war against the United States, China regularly supplied North Vietnam with roughly half a million tonnes of rice annually, as well as soap, cloth and other essential commodities. In 1978, such aid ceased, funding was withdrawn from some 70 industrial projects, and supplies of various raw materials, including 300,000 tonnes of fuel oil, were also cut. The departure to China of about 250,000 Vietnamese workers and managers of

Creche.

Chinese descent also had an impact since many were employed in key industries such as mining, fishing and the docks.

Vietnam was also one of the European Community's major recipients of food aid until 1979, receiving substantial amounts of butter oil, milk powder and cereals. This programme, and further grants which had already been planned, were suspended by a decision of the EEC Council of Ministers in July 1979. A cereal grant of 79,000 tonnes was reallocated to the UN High Commissioner for Refugees for distribution to Kampuchean and Vietnamese refugees. In February 1981 all aid, including indirect aid, was suspended by the European foreign ministers, and since then only emergency aid has been granted, in December 1981 and December 1982, for medical and relief supplies. These grants were made despite ASEAN criticism and against the wishes of some member governments, including Britain.

40

Not all countries have ended their programmes. Sweden in 1982 was still providing assistance of US$80m. a year; its largest project, a US$1bn paper mill at Bai Bang, is nearing completion. The French government has provided about US$30m. and raised its allocation by 30% in 1982. Denmark, Belgium, West Germany, Italy and the Netherlands have maintained limited bilateral programmes. The Labour government in Australia is committed to reconsidering its embargo. India continues an aid programme and a number of countries, including India and Japan as well as the USSR, have agreed to reschedule debt payments.

Within international institutions, the United States has led intensive lobbying against aid programmes to Vietnam. In 1982, the IMF refused a request by Vietnam for US$150m. in Special Drawing Rights for balance of payments support, on the grounds that Vietnam had not carried out economic reforms prescribed by the Fund. Western and other Industrial countries in the Organisation of Economic Cooperation and Development (OECD) have made rescheduling of Vietnam's hard currency debts to them (equivalent to about US$650m.) conditional on acceptance of the IMF terms. The UN Development Programme (UNDP) also halved its commitment to a railway modernisation programme. The World Bank and Asian Development Bank are not funding any projects and various programmes of the World Food Programme, UNICEF, the UN Food and Agriculture Organisation and other international organisations have been restricted or blocked.

Even private development and church organisations have come under pressure from the United States government, which in 1981 narrowly failed to prevent the Mennonites from shipping 250 tonnes of wheat flour to Vietnam. The principal private funding agencies working in Vietnam are Oxfam (UK), Oxfam (Belgique), CARITAS (Germany), the World Council of Churches, the Catholic International Cooperation for Development and Solidarity (CIDSE), and the American Friends Service Committee. Several, including Oxfam and CAFOD in Britain, have asked their governments and the EEC to resume humanitarian aid. Despite the widespread corruption of the Vietnamese administration,

Craft workshop.

these agencies generally agree that their own programmes have been administered effectively and without misappropriation, a view shared by a mission sent out in 1978 by the Commission of the European Communities.

The Role of the Superpowers

The United States provided no development assistance to Vietnam after 1975, nor have diplomatic relations been resumed. Since 1975 American policy can reasonably be described as vindictive. The immense damage caused to Vietnam and to its people by American policies during the war has not deflected successive American administrations from pursuing a punitive strategy designed to isolate Vietnam from contacts with the Western world and stifle its economic development, without consideration of the further suffering this may involve for the Vietnamese people. After the war, both governments made some attempt to restore relations, but each then imposed conditions which caused talks to founder. Initially, they were held up by the Vietnamese demand that reconstruction aid should be linked to diplomatic recognition and over the American insistence that all missing American servicemen should be accounted for before diplomatic relations and trade or aid terms were discussed. Then, in 1977, Congress imposed prohibitions on US aid to Vietnam. In an effort to break the impasse, in July 1978, the Vietnamese government dropped all preconditions to the normalisation process, but, although negotiations were resumed, in September of that year they were overtaken by America's decision to normalise and strengthen ties with China and by the outbreak of hostilities between Vietnam and Kampuchea.

Following President Reagan's election in 1981, American policy became even more uncompromising. Not only were trade and economic relations severed: American officials stated they would use the 'food weapon' to 'bleed' Vietnam into submission. 'We will seek, if we can,' declared Assistant Secretary of State John Holdridge in 1981, 'to find ways to increase the political, economic and, yes, military pressures on Vietnam, working with others in ways which will bring about, we hope, some change in Hanoi's attitude towards the situation.'

The People's Republic of China has followed a similar policy. China was not willing to accept a militarily and politically assertive Vietnam, competing for influence in South East Asia. In Peking's view, Vietnam's alliance with the Soviet Union not only provided the USSR with a base from which to exercise influence in Asia, but threatened China itself with encirclement. Although the alliances have altered, the political choices before Vietnam and Kampuchea—and for that matter, the South East Asian region as a whole—are once more being defined by the strategic interests and conflicts of interest of the superpowers.

Enforced Dependence

The Vietnamese government is reputed to be an uncomfortably obstinate ally. Nevertheless, its ties with the USSR are unquestionably close to the point which makes a degree of economic and military dependence certain. Even during the war, the North Vietnamese government favoured the Soviet Union over China, and since 1975 the USSR and the Soviet bloc countries have continued to supply the bulk of Vietnam's military and economic aid. Facing a disastrous economic situation, and deteriorating relations with China and Kampuchea as well as the United States, Vietnam joined CMEA in 1978 and shortly afterwards concluded a twenty-five year treaty of friendship and cooperation with the Soviet Union. At least temporarily, this ended Vietnam's attempts to avoid alignment in the Sino-Soviet dispute and remain flexible vis-à-vis the non-communist world. Since then, the stategy of isolation pursued by China and the United States, with their allies, has driven Vietnam closer, from weakness, towards the Soviet Union. Though no exact figures have been made available, the IMF estimated that in 1981 alone the

USSR granted Vietnam US$560m. in economic aid and, according to Washington sources, provided military assistance valued at some US$300m. Projects to construct fertiliser plants and a power station are being completed, funded by long-term loans. About 6,000 Russians are working in Vietnam, in addition to several thousand East Europeans and Cubans. A high proportion are military advisers, though others are involved in oil exploration off the Vietnamese coast and in education. Educational reforms in 1983 will make Russian the second language for half Vietnam's secondary school students, in preference to English and French (25% each). At least 10,000 Vietnamese go to the USSR every year for training of some kind, or as contract workers.

By a second agreement, signed in 1981, which covers the volume of goods exchanged between the two countries, Vietnam has pledged to increase exports of rubber, coffee, spices, timber and handicraft products to help cover its huge trade deficit. This means that Vietnam will follow a development model based on the export of unprocessed agricultural goods or light industrial products, exchanged for high value-added imports of industrial equipment. These goods will be financed partly by contracts to send Vietnamese to work in the USSR, an arrangement that might exacerbate the shortage of skilled labour within Vietnam. The USSR has rarely provided its allies in the Third World with the range of resources they need for autonomous development. In Vietnam too, its assistance is apparently concentrated in the spheres of military aid and heavy industrial goods. It has made relatively minor contributions to health and social services.

At the same time, Vietnam's international isolation has placed the entire burden for its support upon communist economies which have severe problems of their own, and heavy commitments in other countries like Cuba and Angola. There is no evidence that Soviet bloc economic aid has decreased but, according to some reports, East European members of CMEA have complained about the scale of assistance Vietnam requires, and it is known that the USSR has not been satisfied that its aid has been used effectively.

Soviet aid is now tied far more than in the past to specific projects, and CMEA pressure may have accelerated the Vietnamese government's decision to introduce the recent economic reforms.

Despite the country's economic difficulties, Vietnam's armed forces and military power continue to increase, and to be supported by the USSR, which uses the military base of Cam Ranh Bay in particular to maintain a naval and air presence in the region. Some of the increased military spending of the ASEAN countries is due to their concern about Soviet influence, which has also given the United States reason to increase military aid to its own allies. The dangers of militarisation in the region will grow while the issue of Kampuchea remains unsettled, since, for as long as Vietnam feels that it is threatened across its Western border by any unsympathetic Kampuchean government, it will strengthen its military alliance with the Soviet Union—and for so long as it does so, China will feel threatened in its turn.

5. Conclusion

If there is to be a solution to the problem of Kampuchea and the impoverishment of Vietnam's people, it will require the consent of the United States, the Soviet Union and China, whose antagonism in this area of the world has continued to make an independent settlement unattainable. Each of the superpowers has been guilty of maximising its own strategic influence in the area at the expense of all other considerations. The result has been wholly destructive. It has set back the development of all countries in the region and crippled the Indo-Chinese economies. It has increased the likelihood of war. It has also caused extremes of suffering. Underlying all discussion of the future is the brutal fact that, while the United States and the Soviet Union, and also China, persist in imposing their political interests over those of the nations which are directly concerned, the region will remain in crisis. It is not in Vietnam's power at present, whether alone, or together with the Kampucheans, or together with the ASEAN governments, to resolve the major problems dividing the region.

The most likely source of creative diplomatic initiatives on Kampuchea is ASEAN. The Vietnamese and ASEAN governments have a common interest in seeing stability in the area for their own economic development, and have a common fear, as small countries, of superpower involvement. Although there are differences in outlook, all, including Thailand, see Chinese domination of the region as a long-term threat and do not consider that it is in their interest to weaken Vietnam permanently. All, including the government in Hanoi, also share the view that long-term dependence on the USSR is not in Vietnam's interest. Vietnam's economic development rather requires a reduction in its military commitments and a return to the flexible relations which governed its foreign policy until 1978.

To be successful, a resolution of the problem of Kampuchea must secure the rights of the people of Kampuchea to sovereignty and independence, and guarantee Vietnam's own security, at present threatened along its lengthy Western frontier as well as from the North. To achieve these two aims, the Vietnamese army must eventually withdraw, permitting the establishment of an independent government freely chosen by the Kampuchean people. Free elections are also the best guarantee *against* any return to power of the Khmer Rouge, hatred and fear of whom has perhaps been the principal reason why resistance within Kampuchea to Vietnam's military occupation has not until now been extensive. If Vietnam remains in military occupation of Kampuchea, however, resistance can be expected to increase. This would strengthen the influence of the Khmer Rouge, which remains militarily the only opposition force at present dangerous to the Vietnamese army. Over a longer period, the growth of Kampuchean nationalism would also, if focussed against Vietnam, undermine the security along Vietnam's border which the occupation of Kampuchea currently assures.

The policies of the United States, China and the ASEAN nations—as well as those of the European governments—are based at present upon the assumption that Vietnam can be coerced rather than persuaded to take a different view of its national interest in Kampuchea and in the region. There is no evidence, however, either in Vietnam's recent history or in the histories of the men who govern it, which suggests that they will yield either to military violence or to economic deprivation. It is far more likely that isolation and

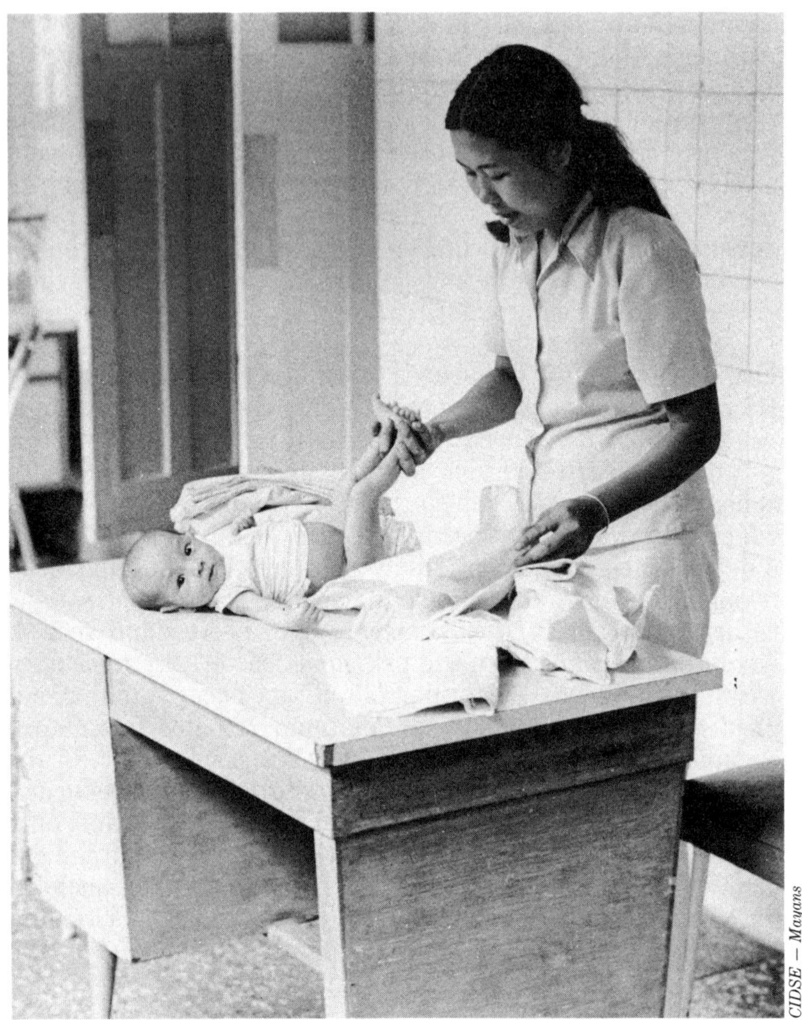

Children's hospital, Ho Chi Minh Ville.

international indifference to their problems will cause the
Vietnamese leadership to harden themselves, and harden the
population they govern, to the sufferings that may be
imposed upon them. Very few observers believe there is any
prospect of driving Vietnam out of Kampuchea or

50

threatening Hanoi into taking a more conciliatory stance towards neighbouring states.

The embargo on all forms of aid, including food and humanitarian aid, is particularly questionable. Vietnam is the only country excluded by the EEC on political grounds from access to humanitarian aid, and it must be asked whether it is morally defensible to penalise children, the sick and those least able to support themselves for actions taken by their governments. In the context of Vietnam's recent history, the strategy becomes even more unjust. The people of Indo-China need aid on the scale that they do very largely because of the war which the United States promoted and other Western governments supported between 1949 and 1975. Moreover, an embargo on humanitarian and food aid will certainly not cause Hanoi to withdraw from Kampuchea.

On the other hand, 'bleeding' Vietnam may well drive its government further into dependence on the Soviet Union. While the Soviet Union has proved able to assist its allies militarily, and can maintain or even increase Vietnam's military strength in the region, its international record in the fields of economic and social development is not impressive. Reliance upon the Soviet Union as an economic partner is therefore a risky option for Vietnam. In the longer term, it is also difficult to see what advantages will accrue to the West from creating an economically weak, militarily powerful and beleaguered Vietnam, dependent for its survival upon the Soviet Union. If peace and the economic development of the region are what the West is seeking to achieve, other policies will be needed.

Under these circumstances, and given the fact that a settlement of the problem of Kampuchea may take years to achieve, the future of the people of Vietnam—and of Indo-China—is bleak. There is a strong case for increasing medical and educational assistance, some forms of food aid, and aid which will increase production and self-sufficiency at local level inside Vietnam. In formulating attitudes towards Indo-China, and towards Vietnam in particular, British and European policy should recognise the degree to which, in recent history, the peoples of the area have been denied all choice or control over their lives by the policies and interests of outside governments. Immense suffering has been caused. The region remains in acute crisis. While the Vietnamese army continues to occupy Kampuchea, no fundamental shift of attitude can be expected from Europe. Nevertheless, European and British policy should recognise the underlying causes of the crisis, and confirm the principle that peoples, including the people of Vietnam, should not intentionally be made to suffer for the failings and the ambitions of other, or even their own, governments.

Books and Documents

Books and Documents

Amnesty International - *Arrest and Trial of Priests and Lay Catholics in Viet Nam*, August 1983, London, roneo.
Bull, David - *The Poverty of Diplomacy: Kampuchea and the Outside World*, OXFAM Public Affairs Unit, Oxford, 1983
Burchett, Wilfred - *The China-Cambodia-Vietnam Triangle*, Zed Press, London, 1981
Cheung Ka-hing - *Kampuchea: Historical and Global Context of the Conflict*, Centre for the Progress of Peoples/Plough Publications, Hong Kong, 1981
Constitution of the Socialist Republic of Viet Nam, Foreign Languages Publishing House, Hanoi, 1981
Hsu, Victor - *The Indo-China Conflicts: Basic Elements*, Commission of the Churches on International Affairs, World Council of Churches, Switzerland, nd.
Indochina Resource Center - *A Time to Heal: the Effects of War on Vietnam, Laos, Cambodia and America*, Washington DC, 1976
Maclear, Michael - *The Ten Thousand Day War: Vietnam 1945-1975*, St Martin's Press, New York, 1981
Shawcross, William - *Sideshow: Kissinger, Nixon and the Destruction of Cambodia*, Fontana, 1980
Thich Nhat Hanh - *Vietnam: The Lotus in the Sea of Fire*, Fellowship of Reconciliation, New York, 1967

Wain, Barry - *The Refused: The Agony of the Indochina Refugees*,
    Dow Jones Publishing Company, Hong Kong, 1981
What is Happening in Indochina?, British Council of Churches
    and the Commission for International Justice and Peace,
    London, 1979

A useful booklist on recent publications on the war in Vietnam
can also be obtained from The National Book League, 45 East
Hill, London SW18 2QZ.

Reports

Amnesty International, *Report of an International Mission to the
    Socialist Republic of Viet Nam, 10-21 December 1979* (1981)
Christian Conference of Asia, *Indochina Consortium Visit to Laos
    and Vietnam*, Singapore (1981)
CIDSE, various reports of visits
Committee on Development and Co-operation of the European
    Parliament, *The Granting of Emergency Aid to Vietnam*
    (Document 1-1270/82, 18 February 1983)
Finnish Inquiry Commission, *Kampuchea in the Seventies*,
    Helsinki (1982)

Journals and Periodicals (in English)

AMPO - Japan Asia Quarterly Review, PO Box 5250, Tokyo
    International, Japan
Indochina Issues, 120 Maryland Avenue, N.E., Washington DC,
    20002.
Journal of Contemporary Asia, PO Box 49010, Stockholm 49,
    Sweden
South East Asia Chronicle, PO Box 4000-D, Berkeley, California
    94704
Vietnam Courier, 46 Tran Hung Dao, Hanoi, SRV